Keeping Your *Promises* to Your Family

Dr. Tony Evans

Keeping Your *Promises* to Your Family

There are no shortcuts to building a healthy, loving, and caring family. It requires time, tears, hard work, and sacrifice. It means putting others first.

———————————

Love one another...as members of one family—
giving precedence and showing honor to one another.
Romans 12:10 AMP

*W*e have one block of time in which to nurture our marriages and build our families: Today. Seize it!

———————————

You are joined together with peace through the Spirit, so make every effort to continue together in this way.
Ephesians 4:3 NCV

DECEMBER 31

Many people moan, "My spouse and I are so different." That's great! If the two of you were exactly alike, one of you would be unnecessary.

But for Adam no suitable helper was found. So the Lord God...made a woman...and he brought her to the man.
Genesis 2:20-22 NIV

J A N U A R Y   2

*D*o you and your mate ever wonder "Whatever happened to the good old days when we used to...?" The next time the question comes up, don't go any further until the two of you answer it!

———————————————

My lover spoke and said to me, "Arise, my darling, my beautiful one, and come with me."
Song of Songs 2:10 NIV

D E C E M B E R   3 0

*A*ccording to the Bible, marriage is a covenant: a divinely established, legally binding relationship between two parties who agree to live within a structure of authority.

The Lord is acting as the witness between you and the wife of your youth,...she is your partner, the wife of your marriage covenant.
Malachi 2:14 NIV

J A N U A R Y   3

It will take a large part of eternity to discover all the blessings that a thousand generations of godly mothers have made possible for their children.

He is the faithful God, keeping his covenant of love to a thousand generations of those who love him and keep his commands.
Deuteronomy 7:9 NIV

DECEMBER 29

$\mathcal{G}$od expects to be a functional part of your marriage and family. He isn't interested in a courtesy nod; He wants to run the whole show.

It is God who is at work in you, enabling you both to will and to work for his good pleasure.
Philippians 2:13 NRSV

JANUARY 4

$\mathcal{M}$en, date your wives. Don't just say, "What do you want to do tonight?" That is not a date! You didn't do that when you were trying to win her. Take the initiative. Set it all up. Plan a special time.

Arise, come, my darling; my beautiful one, come with me.
Song of Songs 2:13 NIV

D E C E M B E R   2 8

A little girl once asked her grandmother, "Why is your wedding ring so thick?" "Because in my day, they were made to last." That is the way God meant marriage to be—solid, binding, enduring.

"A man shall leave his father and mother and be joined to his wife, and the two shall become one flesh." So they are no longer two, but one flesh. Therefore what God has joined together, let no one separate.
Mark 10:7-9 NIV

J A N U A R Y   5

Pray for an army of men in the minority community who will become the faithful, loving husbands and fathers God wants them to be.

And pray in the Spirit on all occasions with all kinds of prayers and requests. With this in mind, be alert and always keep on praying for all the saints.
Ephesians 6:18 NIV

D E C E M B E R   2 7

There are many single parents in our communities, mostly mothers. I cannot imagine a greater challenge. We need to support and encourage them. Single parent, God has a special measure of grace for you.

My grace is sufficient for you, for my power is made perfect in weakness.
2 Corinthians 12:9 NIV

J A N U A R Y   6

A healthy dose of biblical marriage principles is the best antidote to divorce.

If the Lord doesn't build the house,
the builders are working for nothing.
Psalm 127:1 NCV

DECEMBER 26

$\mathcal{A}$s a wife submits to the authority of her husband, God's blessing is free to flow from the husband to his wife, and from her to the children.

You wives must submit to your husbands' leadership in the same way you submit to the Lord.
Ephesians 5:22 TLB

J A N U A R Y   7

*D*oes Christ have the glory in your home?
God wants His Son to be pre-eminent in
everything—including your home.

---

*He is the head of the body, the church, who is
the beginning, the firstborn from the dead, that
in all things He may have the pre-eminence.*
Colossians 1:18 NKJV

D E C E M B E R   2 5

*L*ike a diligent father, God will discipline us
when He cannot get our attention
and respect any other way.

My child, do not regard lightly the discipline of the Lord,
or lose heart when you are punished by him; for the
Lord disciplines those whom he loves, and chastises
every child whom he accepts.
Hebrews 12:5,6 NRSV

J A N U A R Y   8

Is there anything about your marriage or your family life that cannot be accounted for in merely human terms? Something that can only be explained by the power of God? Point that out to your children.

———————————

Now to him who is able to do immeasurably more than all we ask or imagine, according to his power that is at work within us, to him be glory...throughout all generations, for ever and ever!
Ephesians 3:20,21 NIV

D E C E M B E R   2 4

*W*hen a husband or wife tells me, "I'm doing the best I can under the circumstances," my advice is "Get out from under them!"

If you make the Most High your dwelling—even the Lord, who is my refuge—then no harm will befall you, no disaster will come near your tent.
Psalm 91:9,10 NIV

J A N U A R Y   9

*D*ad, be your teen-age daughter's spiritual protector. She needs you not only to evaluate her choice of dates, but to help her identify the spiritual qualities she should look for in a young man.

———————————————

Fathers,...raise them with the training
and teaching of the Lord.
Ephesians 6:4 NCV

D E C E M B E R   2 3

A husband's giving of himself to his wife needs to take place every day in small as well as big ways, not just in rare heroic moments.

Always aim to show kindness and seek to do good to one another.
1 Thessalonians 5:15 AMP

JANUARY 10

*S*atan's strategy was to turn Adam into a passive man and Eve into an aggressive woman so that God's pattern for marriage and family would be reversed. But you have a chance to set things right in your home! Ask God for the wisdom and strength to do it.

Submit yourselves, then, to God.
Resist the devil, and he will flee from you.
James 4:7 NIV

D E C E M B E R   2 2

*J*f your marriage is less than ideal, do not
let it deteriorate a moment longer.
Make today the turning point.

———————————————

*If you love someone you will be loyal
to him no matter what the cost.*
1 Corinthians 13:7 TLB

JANUARY 11

*A*s Christian parents, let's make sure our homes are launching pads from which our children may take off and soar for God.

They that wait upon the Lord shall renew their strength; they shall mount up with wings as eagles; they shall run, and not be weary; and they shall walk, and not faint.
Isaiah 40:31 KJV

DECEMBER 21

*E*ven if your children's gifts and talents are
not the ones you would have chosen for them,
they are the gifts God has chosen for them.

There are different kinds of gifts, but the same Spirit.
All these are the work of one and the same Spirit, and
he gives them to each one, just as he determines.
1 Corinthians 12:4,11 NIV

J A N U A R Y   1 2

$\mathcal{E}$very time I think of the wonderful men and women of God in our churches, I am reminded that the battle is ours to win!

_____

In all these things we are more than conquerors through him who loved us.
Romans 8:37 NIV

D E C E M B E R   2 0

$\mathcal{L}$ove is doing a thoughtful deed for your spouse or children with no expectation of return.

_____

Love each other...and take delight in each other.
Romans 12:10 NRSV

J A N U A R Y   1 3

Singleness is a calling from God, just as marriage is a calling from God. Both are equally valuable.

We are not all the same. God gives some the gift of a husband or wife, and others he gives the gift of being able to stay happily unmarried.
1 Corinthians 7:7 NIV

D E C E M B E R   1 9

A wife can play a great supporting role
to make it easier for her husband
to fulfill his leadership role.

_____

In the same way, their wives are
to be women worthy of respect.
1 Timothy 3:11 NIV

JANUARY 14

*N*o sane woman wants to be delivered from a husband who loves her 24 hours a day, who embraces, compliments, and encourages her.

And you husbands, show the same kind of love to your wives as Christ showed to the Church when he died for her. In this same way, husbands ought to love their wives as their own bodies. He who loves his wife loves himself.
Ephesians 5:28 NIV

DECEMBER 18

$\mathcal{I}$ know that true love and forgiveness work in families. I have seen them heal hurts and bring hearts back together.

Be kind and compassionate to one another, forgiving each other, just as in Christ God forgave you.
Ephesians 4:32 NIV

J A N U A R Y   1 5

There is nothing better than grandparents who can tell you what wonderful things God has done for them personally throughout their years of experience with Him. Develop your faith now, and you will have a testimony like that when you are old.

———————————————

We will tell to the coming generation the glorious deeds of the Lord, and his might, and the wonders that he has done.
Psalm 78:4 NRSV

DECEMBER 17

The spiritual strength of your marriage is determined by the degree to which you keep the vow of unconditional love that you made to your partner at the wedding altar.

Above all, clothe yourselves with love, which binds everything together in perfect harmony.
Colossians 3:14 NRSV

J A N U A R Y   1 6

$\mathcal{A}$t any point, a Christian husband or wife can start over by simply praying, "Lord, I want to be Your kind of husband (wife). I want to honor my spouse and make home a priority."

For it is God who works in you to will and to act according to his good purpose.
Philippians 2:13 NIV

D E C E M B E R   1 6

$\mathcal{T}$he aim of love is to promote spiritual growth—
in ourselves and others, but especially
in our families.

---

*From him the whole body...grows and builds
itself up in love, as each part does its work.*
Ephesians 4:16 NIV

JANUARY 17

Pamper your wife and make her feel like somebody special. After all, she is!

_____

How beautiful you are and how pleasing,
O love, with your delights!
Song of Songs 7:6 NIV

DECEMBER 15

*H*ow does a husband love his wife like Christ loved the church? *Sacrificially!*

Husbands, love your wives, just as Christ loved the church and gave himself up for her.
Ephesians 5:25 NIV

JANUARY 18

*W*hatever you are planning to do, ask yourself if Jesus would do that. Remember, you take Him with you wherever you go.

_____

Whatever you do, in word or deed, do everything in the name of the Lord Jesus.
Colossians 3:17 NRSV

DECEMBER 14

In Scripture, honor and respect are first spoken of in regard to parents.

_____

Honor your father and your mother, so that your days may be long in the land that the Lord your God is giving you.
Exodus 20:12 NRSV

J A N U A R Y   1 9

*A*gape love is different from other loves because it is acting on someone else's behalf without expecting anything in return.

_____

Love is patient; love is kind....
It does not insist on its own way.
1 Corinthians 13:4,5 NRSV

D E C E M B E R   1 3

The mate God gave you was created to fit together with you in marriage.

_____

And the Lord God said, "It isn't good for man to be alone; I will make a companion for him, a helper suited to his needs."
Genesis 2:18 TLB

JANUARY 20

Whatever our marital status, the Bible warns us to run from immorality. The idea is to skate where the ice is thickest, not thinnest.

Flee from sexual immorality. All other sins a man commits are outside his body, but he who sins sexually sins against his own body.
1 Corinthians 6:18 NIV

D E C E M B E R   1 2

Our daughters should not be satisfied with any man who does not respect them enough to put their comfort above his own.

Learn to put aside your own desires so that you will become patient and godly, gladly letting God have his way with you.
2 Peter 1:6 TLB

J A N U A R Y   2 1

*D*ad, did you know that God has made you the priest of your home? You are a chosen man.

_____

But you are a chosen people, a royal priesthood,...
a people belonging to God, that you may declare
the praises of him who called you out of
darkness into his wonderful light.
1 Peter 2:9 NIV

D E C E M B E R   1 1

$\mathcal{T}$he black community desperately needs strong male leaders—men who will serve as mentors and role models to young men and women.

———————————

Let your light so shine before men, that they may see your good works, and glorify your Father which is in heaven.
Matthew 5:16 KJV

J A N U A R Y   2 2

A husband must cleave to his wife.
The word cleave means "to stick like glue"
or "to attach oneself in a viselike grip."

_____

*This is what I have asked of God for you: that you
will be...knit together by strong ties of love.*
Colossians 2:2 TLB

D E C E M B E R   1 0

A wife's respect for her husband should have nothing to do with his success or failure in his job. She is to respect him because of his God-given position.

---

*Admire, praise, be devoted to,
deeply love and enjoy [your husband].*
1 Peter 3:2 *AMP*

J A N U A R Y   2 3

Single women should keep their standards high and be patient. Better 10 years with the right man than 30 years with the wrong one.

But be sure...that you are living as God intended, marrying or not marrying in accordance with God's direction and help, and accepting whatever situation God has put you into.
1 Corinthians 7:17 TLB

D E C E M B E R   9

Prayer is the single most important aspect of the Christian life because it is foundational. Everything else builds on it.

Pray in the Spirit on all occasions with all kinds of prayers and requests.
Ephesians 6:18 NIV

JANUARY 24

Do you pray for what you want, or what God wants? Your motivation determines the answer you will receive from heaven.

And this is the boldness we have in him, that if we ask anything according to his will, he hears us. And if we know that he hears us in whatever we ask, we know that we have obtained the requests made of him.
1 John 5:14,15 NRSV

DECEMBER 8

$\mathcal{F}$athers need to know and to tell their sons that big boys *do* cry. Strong Christian men do not ever need to be ashamed of their tears.

_____

They all wept as they embraced him and kissed him.
Acts 20:37 NIV

J A N U A R Y   2 5

Handling money well is critical to the health of a marriage. We promised our love to our mates "till death do us part," not "till *debt* do us part."

You cannot serve both God and Money.
Matthew 6:24 NIV

DECEMBER 7

*g*od expects parents to be honest about
their shortcomings and limitations.
Only then will their example have
credibility with their children.

---

*I tell you the truth, unless you change and become
like little children, you will never enter the kingdom
of heaven. Therefore, whoever humbles himself like
this child is the greatest in the kingdom of heaven.*
Matthew 18:3,4 NIV

J A N U A R Y   2 6

$\mathcal{I}$f you want your children to love Christ,
you will have to be *passionate* about Him!

———————————————

*Whom have I in heaven but you? And there is nothing
on earth that I desire other than you.... God is the
strength of my heart and my portion forever.*
Psalm 73:25,26 NRSV

D E C E M B E R   6

There is not a marriage in the world that cannot work once the two parties involved decide to do things God's way.

As you received Christ Jesus the Lord, so continue to live in him. Keep your roots deep in him and have your lives built on him.
Colossians 2:6,7 NCV

J A N U A R Y   2 7

When a wife willingly submits to her husband's authority, she is not just saying yes to him. She is saying yes to the Lord.

_____

Submit yourselves therefore to God.... Humble yourselves before the Lord, and he will exalt you.
James 4:7,10 NRSV

D E C E M B E R   5

Spend time with married couples and families who have it together spiritually. If you hang around those in spiritual darkness too long, the dark doesn't seem so dark anymore.

But if we walk in the light, as he is in the light, we have fellowship with one another, and the blood of Jesus, his Son, purifies us from all sin.
1 John 1:7 NIV

J A N U A R Y   2 8

*W*hat kind of aroma does your home give off?
Make sure it's a sweet fragrance to God.

———————————

*For we are to God the aroma of Christ among
those who are being saved and those who
are perishing..., the fragrance of life.*
2 Corinthians 2:15,16 NIV

D E C E M B E R   4

*C*onflicts in marriage should not destroy the union. They should show the power of Christ within us.

———————————————

I pray that out of his glorious riches he may strengthen you with power through his Spirit in your inner being.
Ephesians 3:16 NIV

J A N U A R Y   2 9

*M*aking our marriages work involves
spiritual warfare. We must defeat Satan
in his attempts to overcome us.

_____

*Put on the full armor of God so that you can
take your stand against the devil's schemes.*
Ephesians 6:11 NIV

D E C E M B E R   3

The first step in building good marital and family communication is being honest with each other.

Therefore each of you must put off falsehood and speak truthfully..., for we are all members of one body.
Ephesians 4:25 NIV

J A N U A R Y   3 0

If your children ask why others can live bad lives without apparent consequences, remind them that they left off one important word: *Yet*. God does not always settle His accounts right away.

_____

For the wages of sin is death, but the gift of God is eternal life in Christ Jesus our Lord.
Romans 6:23 NIV

D E C E M B E R   2

*I*t does not take a lot of money to have a great date with your spouse. What makes a date a date is the excitement of doing something together.

Awake, north wind, and come, south wind! Blow on my garden, that its fragrance may spread abroad. Let my lover come into his garden and taste its choice fruits.
Song of Songs 4:16 NIV

J A N U A R Y   3 1

*C*an you remember that time in your marriage when love ruled? It can be that way again!

Let him kiss me with the kisses of his mouth—
for your love is more delightful than wine.
Song of Songs 1:2 NIV

D E C E M B E R   1

*T*ry this experiment. For one week, do not say anything to your spouse or children unless it is wholesome and will contribute to the person and his or her spiritual growth. See how much of a difference it makes to your family.

Say only what is good and helpful to those you are talking to, and what will give them a blessing.
Ephesians 4:29 TLB

F E B R U A R Y   1

*E*ven when sinfulness appears in the life of someone you love, the loving thing to do is to reject it.

———————————

If someone is caught in a sin, you who are spiritual should restore him gently.
Galatians 6:1 NIV

N O V E M B E R   3 0

*I*t only takes a few minutes to get married, but it takes a lifetime to keep a marriage thriving.

May God who gives patience, steadiness, and encouragement help you to live in complete harmony with each other—each with the attitude of Christ toward the other.
Romans 15:5 TLB

FEBRUARY 2

*T*rue love wants the one who is loved to be right before God. That is why true love sometimes disciplines and corrects.

In response to all he has done for us, let us outdo each other in being helpful and kind to each other and in doing good.
Hebrews 10:24 TLB

N O V E M B E R   2 9

A mistaken message given to women today is that they can do and have it all: home, family, career, and more. But the human body can only do so much. You must decide what you can do and eliminate what you cannot.

That our God...may fulfill every good purpose
of yours and every act prompted by your faith.
2 Thessalonians 1:11 NIV

F E B R U A R Y 3

$\mathcal{T}$wo people who are outdoing each other to sacrifice for the sake of the other will have a dynamic love and a dynamic testimony for the Lord!

_____

Love each other...and take delight in honoring each other.
Romans 12:10 TLB

N O V E M B E R   2 8

*P*arents, the battle to raise godly children is ours to win—and we have God's promise of a good result if we hang in there.

Let us not be weary in well doing: for in due season we shall reap, if we faint not.
Galatians 6:9 KJV

FEBRUARY 4

*G*od calls older women who have their homes together to help and encourage younger women who may want to give up on their homes.

Tell the older women to be reverent in behavior,...
so that they may encourage the young women.
Titus 2:3,4 NRSV

N O V E M B E R   2 7

*I*f we follow God's principles, *our families can make it*. There is real hope for us, because God's power is far greater than the influences that surround us.

———————————

Greater is he that is in you, than he that is in the world.
1 John 4:4 KJV

F E B R U A R Y   5

*L*ive in such a way that God could say to your children, "Do you want to know how I designed love and marriage to work? Follow your parents' example."

———————————————

Follow my example, as I follow the example of Christ.
1 Corinthians 11:1 NIV

N O V E M B E R   2 6

*I*f we look for what God is trying to teach us through the mate He has given us, our energy will be invested in growing rather than griping.

———————————————

I am the Lord your God, who teaches you to do what is good, who leads you in the way you should go.
Isaiah 48:17 NCV

F E B R U A R Y   6

$\mathcal{I}$f you want your children to get excited about what God can do in their lives, let them see God doing something exciting in your life.

Your power and goodness, Lord, reach to the highest heavens. You have done such wonderful things. Where is there another God like you?
Psalm 71:19 TLB

N O V E M B E R   2 5

*I*f you are a parent, you are qualified to teach your children. No one else has the knowledge you have. More than anyone else, you know what makes your child tick.

My child, keep your father's commandment,
and do not forsake your mother's teaching.
Proverbs 6:20 NRSV

F E B R U A R Y   7

A good woman is worth a lifetime of careful study—that is how long it will take you to really know your wife.

———————————————

Live happily with the woman you love through the fleeting days of life, for the wife God gives you is your best reward down here for all your earthly toil.
Ecclesiastes 9:9 TLB

N O V E M B E R   2 4

A husband's craving for respect rivals his need for love. Both are essential.

A man must love his wife as part of himself; and the wife must see to it that she deeply respects her husband.
Ephesians 5:33 NIV

F E B R U A R Y   8

One of the best things you can do for your children is to let them experience the consequences of their actions.

_____

Be happy, young man, while you are young.... Follow the ways of your heart and whatever your eyes see, but know that for all these things God will bring you to judgment.
Ecclessiastes 11:9 NIV

N O V E M B E R   2 3

*O*ffer your child to the Lord the first thing each morning. Allow Him to be responsible for the life of your child throughout the day.

———————————————

You know when I sit and when I rise;
you perceive my thoughts from afar.
Psalm 139:2 NIV

F E B R U A R Y   9

*G*race should make us grateful creatures. Instead of taking things for granted, we should be grateful for the roof over our heads, the food on our table, the mate beside us, and the children around us.

―――――――――

For you know the grace of our Lord Jesus Christ, that though he was rich, yet for your sakes he became poor, so that you through his poverty might become rich.
2 Corinthians 8:9 NIV

N O V E M B E R   2 2

$\mathcal{P}$rayer needs to be our first response to a need,
not our last resort.

Pray without ceasing.
1 Thessalonians 5:17 KJV

FEBRUARY 10

*B*e sure to show your spouse today that you appreciate him or her. Like the old saying goes, "Send me flowers while I'm still living."

As for man, his days are like grass,
he flourishes like a flower of the field.
Psalm 103:15 NIV

NOVEMBER 21

*Y*our circumstances are never the last word
as long as God is on the scene.

_____

*And God is able to make all grace abound toward you,
that you, always having all sufficiency in all things,
may have an abundance for every good work.
2 Corinthians 9:8 NKJV*

F E B R U A R Y   1 1

*N*ever trade something that only God can give you for even the best that society can give you.

Anyone who chooses to be a friend of the world becomes an enemy of God.
James 4:4 NIV

NOVEMBER 20

God has commanded that marriages be permanent; therefore, we know that He will give to each believer the ability to accomplish His will for his or her marriage.

May the God of peace...equip you with everything good for doing his will, and may he work in us what is pleasing to him.
Hebrews 13:20,21 NIV

F E B R U A R Y   1 2

$\mathcal{I}$f you are God's kind of mother, you will achieve something very significant. You will give God's world something He can be proud of—children who know and honor Him.

_____

She watches over the ways of her household....
Her children rise up and call her blessed;
her husband also, and he praises her:
Proverbs 31:27,28 NKJV

N O V E M B E R   1 9

*W*hen your children see you and your spouse working hard at your marriage instead of just bailing out, they will learn two valuable lessons: the real meaning of commitment, and the beauty and power of forgiveness.

———————————

God, who has called you into fellowship with his Son Jesus Christ our Lord, is faithful.
1 Corinthians 1:9 NIV

F E B R U A R Y   1 3

There are no problems you and your mate cannot solve if you learn God's guidelines for making your differences complementary rather than contradictory.

———————————

Jesus looked at them and said, "With man this is impossible, but not with God; all things are possible with God." Mark 10:27 NIV

N O V E M B E R   1 8

*M*en, remember when you were dating your wife
and you could not wait to open the car door for her?
Date her again! Do the little, thoughtful things
that keep the romance alive.

_____

He brings me to the banquet hall, and
everyone can see how much he loves me.
Song of Solomon 2:4 TLB

F E B R U A R Y 1 4

*P*rayer is our way of saying,
"I'm banking on you, God."

---

*Do not be anxious about anything, but in
everything, by prayer and petition, with
thanksgiving, present your requests to God.*
Philippians 4:6 NIV

N O V E M B E R   1 7

*M*y daddy used to tell me, "As long as I am head of this home...," and then he would lay down the rules. "If you don't want that," he would continue, "then you need to live somewhere else. Because as for me and my house, we are going to serve the Lord."

He will command his children and his household after him, and they shall keep the way of the Lord.
Genesis 18:19 KJV

FEBRUARY 15

It is worth it to wait on God, because when He moves, He moves well.

Yet the Lord longs to be gracious to you; he rises to show you compassion. For the Lord is a God of justice. Blessed are all who wait for him!
Isaiah 30:18 NIV

N O V E M B E R   1 6

*G*od gave us marriage to demonstrate what it will be like when we are united with Him.

"A man will...be united to his wife, and the two will become one flesh." This is a profound mystery— but I am talking about Christ and the church.
Ephesians 5:31,32 NIV

FEBRUARY 16

*I*f you can't afford it, don't buy it. Young couples cannot expect to obtain in one year what it took their parents 20 years to accumulate.

———————————

*Keep your lives free from the love of money
and be content with what you have.*
Hebrews 13:5 NIV

N O V E M B E R   1 5

*W*omen, when you consider a man for marriage, remember that before God gave Adam a wife, He gave him responsibility.

The Lord God took the man and put him in the Garden of Eden to work it and take care of it.
Genesis 2:15 NIV

FEBRUARY 17

If a wife is working in order to help meet the financial needs of the home, she is helping her husband do what God told him to do. So when his wife asks for his help in doing what God told her to do, a husband has no right to say, "That's woman's work."

Husbands, in the same way be considerate as you live with your wives.
1 Peter 3:7 NRSV

NOVEMBER 14

*A*n important element of Christian manhood
is the ability to put divine truth into action
at home and on the job.

_____

*Walk worthy of the Lord, fully pleasing Him,
being fruitful in every good work and increasing
in the knowledge of God.*
Colossians 1:10 NKJV

F E B R U A R Y   1 8

*G*od made marriage in such a way that no third party has a right to interfere with the married couple's relationship.

So they are no longer two, but one flesh. Therefore what God has joined together, let no one separate.
Matthew 19:6 NRSV

N O V E M B E R   1 3

*I*f you are in a difficult relationship, don't be discouraged. God wants your marriage to succeed. He is ready to help you and your mate.

_____

*He will yet fill your mouth with laughter
and your lips with shouts of joy.*
Job 8:21 NIV

F E B R U A R Y   1 9

*A*ny sacrifice parents need to make to ensure that they do not lose their kids is worth it. No Christian parent has to surrender his children to the world.

————————————

As you know, we dealt with each one of you like a father with his children, urging and encouraging you and pleading that you lead a life worthy of God.
1 Thessalonians 2:11,12 NRSV

N O V E M B E R   1 2

$\mathcal{W}$oman was created to come alongside man and assist him. She was never meant to bear alone the responsibility for the home and the family.

———————————

Then the Lord God said, "It is not good that the man should be alone; I will make him a helper as his partner."
Genesis 2:18 NRSV

F E B R U A R Y   2 0

*R*emember God while you are young.
Don't grow old with nothing to show for it.

———————————

Remember your creator in the days of your youth,
before the days of trouble come, and the years draw
near when you will say, "I have no pleasure in them."
Ecclesiastes 12:1 NRSV

N O V E M B E R   1 1

A real man behaves in such a way that his family has no choice but to respect him. He *earns* respect from his wife and children. This is very different from simply demanding it.

Whoever pursues righteousness and kindness will find life and honor.
Proverbs 21:21 NRSV

FEBRUARY 21

*M*arriage is a lifetime process of growth, development, and problem-solving. Anyone who believes otherwise has been reading too many fairy tales.

Love...always perseveres.
1 Corinthians 13:6,7 NIV

N O V E M B E R   1 0

*B*iblical submission in marriage reflects a willingness to use your talents, opportunities, and gifts to achieve the goals established jointly for the good of the marriage.

Submit to one another out of reverence for Christ.
Ephesians 5:21 NIV

FEBRUARY 22

Do you want a miracle in your personal life, in your marriage, or in your family? Then you will have to be fervent in your prayer life.

The effectual fervent prayer of
a righteous man availeth much.
James 5:16 KJV

N O V E M B E R   9

*D*iscipline isn't pleasant for anyone, including the discipliner. My father didn't enjoy spanking me, and I certainly did not enjoy being on the receiving end! But my dad's thinking went beyond what would make either of us happy at that moment, to the long-term results.

Discipline your children, and they will give you rest;
they will give delight to your heart.
Proverbs 29:17 NRSV

F E B R U A R Y   2 3

When you wake up in the morning think about what God has done for you that you do not deserve. It will change your whole perspective and put a little joy in your life.

Satisfy us in the morning with your steadfast love, so that we may rejoice and be glad all our days.
Psalm 90:14 NRSV

N O V E M B E R   8

When a husband says, "I have achieved so much," he ought always to add, "because at home I have someone who has enabled me to."

————————————

Remember that in God's plan men and women need each other.
1 Corinthians 11:11 TLB

F E B R U A R Y   2 4

Dad, your job at home is different from Mom's job. Her job is to nourish the home. Yours is to maintain order and harmony in the home.

_____

Above all, clothe yourselves with love, which binds everything together in perfect harmony.
Colossians 3:14 NRSV

NOVEMBER 7

*A*s daunting as it seems, we parents should tell our children to follow our example—and then back up our words by the way we live.

_____

Follow my example, as I follow the example of Christ.
1 Corinthians 11:1 NIV

FEBRUARY 25

*T*he test of commitment does not come when you are winning the game, but when you are losing. It does not take much commitment to be on the winning side. But it takes commitment to stay in the game instead of quitting when the marriage needs work.

Do you not know that in a race all the runners run, but only one gets the prize? Run in such a way as to get the prize.
1 Corinthians 9:24 NIV

N O V E M B E R   6

*A*dam did not have parents. But if he did, he would have left them for Eve.

For this reason a man will leave his father and mother and be united to his wife, and the two will become one flesh.
Ephesians 5:31 NIV

F E B R U A R Y   2 6

The mark of authentic Christian parents is that they are not out to please or impress people, but to do what is best for their children.

_____

People were bringing little children to Jesus to have him touch them, but the disciples rebuked them. When Jesus saw this, he was indignant. He said to them, "Let the little children come to me."
Mark 10:13 NIV

NOVEMBER 5

*F*athers, set the spiritual tone for your household. Assume the responsibility for getting your family to church, and be a leader when you get there.

_____

Choose you this day whom ye will serve;...but as for me and my house, we will serve the Lord.
Joshua 24:15 KJV

F E B R U A R Y   2 7

*W*ives need to know the Scriptures so they can respond to their husbands God's way.

Their delight is in the law of the Lord, and on his law they meditate day and night.
Psalm 1:2 NRSV

N O V E M B E R   4

$\mathcal{M}$arriage is not a man working a wife into his schedule; marriage is a man making his wife his everything!

_____

*Each one of you also must love
his wife as he loves himself.*
Ephesians 5:33 NIV

FEBRUARY 28

*H*usbands need to know the Scriptures so their wives can be confident that their husbands are basing their thinking on God's truth.

_____

I revere your commandments, which I love,
and I will meditate on your statutes.
Psalm 119:48 NRSV

N O V E M B E R   3

*B*iblical love is commitment love. It is not simply how you *feel*. More than that, it is what you *do*.

_____

This is how we know what love is: Jesus Christ laid down his life for us. And we ought to lay down our lives for our brothers.
1 John 3:16 NIV

F E B R U A R Y 2 9

Take each of your children out to breakfast or lunch every month, just to talk about what's going on. This is a great way to really get to know each other.

_____

These commandments...are to be upon your hearts. Impress them on your children. Talk about them when you sit at home and when you walk along the road, when you lie down and when you get up.
Deuteronomy 6:6, 7 NIV

NOVEMBER 2

If a man will leave and cleave the way
God intended, his wife will respond
the way God intended.

---

*I will betroth you in faithfulness, and
you will acknowledge the Lord.*
Hosea 2:20 NIV

MARCH 1

*W*hen you come home at night, is your family better off because you arrived? Think about it before you walk in the door.

Encourage each other to build each other up.
1 Thessalonians 5:11 TLB

N O V E M B E R   1

*S*ometimes single people are given the impression that marriage is the ultimate goal of life for the Christian. That simply is not true.

———————————————

Each one should retain the place in life that the Lord assigned to him and to which God has called him.
1 Corinthians 7:17 NIV

M A R C H   2

God calls children His heritage. Parents are
to raise them to keep His name going,
not just to keep their name going.

_____

Children are a heritage from the Lord,
The fruit of the womb is a reward.
Psalm 127:3 NKJV

O C T O B E R   3 1

If a husband lets his wife know she is loved and makes her feel secure, he will not have to worry about her fulfilling her responsibilities at home.

_____

Husbands,...show consideration for your wives in your life together, paying honor to the woman.
1 Peter 3:7 NRSV

MARCH 3

A husband is responsible for creating a climate in which his wife can flourish.

But the wisdom that comes from heaven is first of all pure; then peace-loving, considerate, submissive, full of mercy and good fruit, impartial and sincere.
James 3:17 NIV

O C T O B E R   3 0

*W*hen God told Adam and Eve to "be fruitful and multiply," He was not just telling them to reproduce look-alikes. He was telling them to pass on *His* image to their children.

So God created man in his own image, in the image of God created he him; male and female created he them. And God blessed them, and God said unto them, "Be fruitful, and multiply, and replenish the earth."
Genesis 1:27,28 KJV

M A R C H   4

*A*ny father worth his salt wants a legacy. If I want grandchildren I can be proud of, I must invest my time to instill my values in my sons and daughters. I have to pass the baton to them.

Fix these words of mine in your hearts and minds....
Teach them to your children, talking about them when
you sit at home and when you walk along the road,
when you lie down and when you get up.
Deuteronomy 11:18,19 NIV

O C T O B E R 2 9

*U*sed improperly, credit cards operate
a lot like sin: enjoy now, pay later.

As they go on their way they are choked by life's worries,
riches and pleasures, and they do not mature.
Luke 8:14 NIV

M A R C H   5

$\mathcal{I}$f you can't afford it, don't buy it. Young couples cannot expect to obtain in one year what it took their parents 20 years to accumulate.

---

*Keep your lives free from the love of money
and be content with what you have.*
Hebrews 13:5 NIV

O C T O B E R   2 8

*D*o something unexpected for your spouse.
Keep your relationship from becoming boring.

Many waters cannot quench love;
rivers cannot wash it away.
Song of Songs 8:7 NIV

M A R C H   6

*I*t takes a lifetime to become totally one flesh in marriage. That is why marriage is "till death do us part."

———————————————

Make my joy complete by being like-minded, having the same love, being one in spirit and purpose.
Philippians 2:2 NIV

O C T O B E R   2 7

Your family will never be perfect. Neither will mine. The important thing is not aiming for perfection, but making sure our families are walking in the right direction.

If we walk in the light, as he is in the light, we have fellowship with one another, and the blood of Jesus, his Son, purifies us from all sin.
1 John 1:7 NIV

M A R C H   7

Families today can be divided into three categories: the haves, the have-nots, and the have-not-yet-paid-for-what-they-haves!

Let no debt remain outstanding, except the continuing debt to love one another, for he who loves his fellowman has fulfilled the law.
Romans 13:8 NIV

OCTOBER 26

$\mathcal{T}$he more time we spend spend giving thanks, the more at home we will feel in God's presence.

No matter what happens, always be thankful, for this is God's will for you who belong to Christ Jesus.
1 Thessalonians 5:18 TLB

M A R C H   8

$\mathcal{I}$n God's design for the family, there is no leader who is not also a lover.

In this same way, husbands ought to love their wives as their own bodies. He who loves his wife loves himself.
Ephesians 5:28 NIV

OCTOBER 25

*M*arriage is an earthly replica of the divine Trinity—three persons who are one: a man, a woman, and the Lord.

_____

As you, Father, are in me and I am in you, may they also be in us,...so that they may be one as we are one. John 17:21,22 NRSV

M A R C H   9

*C*hristian marriage is wonderful, but it is not a cure-all. If your relationship with Christ is not rich and satisfying before marriage, nothing magical will happen when you enter the state of matrimony.

Let the peace of heart which comes from Christ be always present in your hearts and lives...and always be thankful.
Colossians 3:15 TLB

OCTOBER 24

*A*s parents, we need to look beyond our children to our grandchildren and even our great grandchildren. Then we can raise our children with far-reaching, eternal goals in mind.

———————————————

But from everlasting to everlasting the Lord's love is with those who fear him, and his righteousness with their children's children.
Psalm 103:17 NIV

M A R C H   1 0

One great way to strengthen your marriage is to take opportunities to build up your mate in front of others.

———————————

Her husband...praises her: "Many women do noble things, but you surpass them all."
Proverbs 31:28 NIV

OCTOBER 23

*C*hristians should see themselves as servants to others, especially to hurting people and those children in urban areas who don't have the privilege of living with a father and mother.

———————

Whoever wants to become great among
you must be your servant.
Matthew 20:26 NIV

M A R C H   1 1

Do you know why God gives you money?
Because He wants you to use it for eternal
purposes, whether it is the portion you give
to Him or the portion you use for your needs.

_____

*But my God shall supply all your need according
to his riches in glory by Christ Jesus.*
Philippians 4:19 KJV

OCTOBER 22

*W*e must never be content to simply protect our children from the world. We must prepare them to change the world.

Do not conform any longer to the pattern of this world, but be transformed by the renewing of your mind. Then you will be able to test and approve what God's will is—his good, pleasing and perfect will.
Romans 12:2 NIV

M A R C H   1 2

*W*hen a man marries a woman, he is not acquiring a housekeeper. He is gaining a helpmate to fulfill with him God's great purposes for their lives.

And the Lord God said, "It isn't good for man to be alone; I will make a companion for him, a helper suited to his needs."
Genesis 2:18 TLB

O C T O B E R   2 1

*W*hen a woman's circuits are overloaded with the home and the food and the kids, she needs a husband who sympathizes, not criticizes.

The wisdom that comes from heaven is first of all pure; then peace-loving, considerate, submissive, full of mercy and good fruit, impartial and sincere.
James 3:17 NIV

MARCH 13

Sometimes God does not give us the things we ask for because He knows that if He gave them to us now, He would never see them again. Seek the Giver, not His gifts.

But seek first his kingdom and his righteousness, and all these things will be given to you as well.
Matthew 6:33 NIV

O C T O B E R   2 0

$\mathcal{D}$id you know that God never commanded wives to love their husbands? He commanded them to respect their husbands.

The wife must respect her husband.
Ephesians 5:33 NIV

MARCH 14

A wedding ring is much more than a piece of jewelry to place on a finger. It is a symbol of a lifelong, loving commitment.

May your fountain be blessed, and may you rejoice in the wife of your youth.
Proverbs 5:18 *NIV*

OCTOBER 19

A real husband and father knows that wrong is wrong. You can't influence him by pointing out that the crowd is heading in the opposite direction.

Don't copy the behavior and customs of this world, but be a new and different person.
Romans 12:2 TLB

MARCH 15

*D*ad, make sure you hug and kiss your boys as well as your girls. Put your arm around them, and let them know that you love them and that everything is going to be all right.

He is like a father to us, tender and sympathetic to those who reverence him.
Psalm 103:13 TLB

O C T O B E R 1 8

Marriage in a nutshell is leave, cleave, and become one.

Therefore shall a man leave his father and his mother, and shall cleave unto his wife: and they shall be one flesh.
Genesis 2:24 KJV

MARCH 16

*Y*our ability to love faces its hardest test when the ones you are trying to love throw stones at you.

If someone strikes you on one cheek, turn to him the other also.... Do to others as you would have them do to you.
Luke 6:29,31 NIV

OCTOBER 17

$\mathcal{S}$pirit-filled believers know when to submit—
whether in the home, at church, or on the job.

Honor Christ by submitting to each other.
Ephesians 5:21 TLB

M A R C H   1 7

Satan wants to keep husbands and wives from experiencing oneness and unity in their marriage. He knows that if he can keep a couple fighting, their prayers will not reach heaven.

Husbands, in the same way be considerate as you live with your wives...so that nothing will hinder your prayers.
1 Peter 3:7 NIV

OCTOBER 16

*R*aise your children in such a way that, whether they wind up in Baltimore, New York, or Los Angeles when they move away from home, God will be invited to relocate with them.

_____

Train a child in the way he should go, and when he is old he will not turn from it.
Proverbs 22:6 NIV

M A R C H   1 8

God calls men in the church and in the family to take the lead in prayer.

I want men everywhere to lift up holy hands in prayer.
1 Timothy 2:8 NIV

OCTOBER 15

*G*od is the ultimate authority in a marriage, because marriage is a divine institution. Our desires, disagreements, and discontentments are secondary issues.

Be humble and gentle. Be patient with each other, making allowance for each other's faults because of your love.
Ephesians 4:2 TLB

M A R C H   1 9

*M*any Christians really believe that if they just think, work, and plan hard enough, they can get the job done. They forget to depend on God through prayer.

———————————————

Then Jesus told them a parable about their need to pray always and not to lose heart.
Luke 18:1 NRSV

O C T O B E R   1 4

The Bible says we must "give to Caesar," that is, pay our taxes. But Caesar apparently does not trust us; he takes his off the top. The Lord could take His portion out of our income too, but He doesn't work that way. He wants us to offer it to Him.

Then he said to them, "Give to Caesar what is Caesar's, and to God what is God's."
Matthew 22:21 NIV

M A R C H   2 0

*O*ften a wife will ask her husband, "Do you love me?" His answer may be, "You *know* I love you." No she doesn't! You have to keep telling her, keep showing her she is your one-and-only.

———————————————

My command is this: Love each other
as I have loved you.
John 15:12 NIV

O C T O B E R   1 3

The essence of a good teacher is patience. As our children's teachers, we have unlimited opportunities to learn and practice patience.

———————————

Love is patient, love is kind.
1 Corinthians 13:4 NIV

M A R C H   2 1

$\mathcal{M}$en, if you have a woman who fears the Lord, you have a treasure, because she will show that reverence in every area of life. She will raise her children in the fear of the Lord and respect you in the fear of the Lord.

A woman who fears the Lord, she shall be praised.
Proverbs 31:30 NKJV

O C T O B E R   1 2

A noble wife is one who has decided that her home comes first.

A wife of noble character who can find?
She is worth far more than rubies.
Proverbs 31:10 NIV

M A R C H   2 2

*G*od does not invite you to church to hear the preacher or the choir. He invites you to church to meet with Him.

Enter his gates with thanksgiving and his courts with praise; give thanks to him and praise his name.
Psalm 100:4 NIV

OCTOBER 11

$\mathcal{D}$iscipleship in the home requires more than telling someone what to do; it includes enforcing what is right.

_____

For these commands are a lamp, this teaching is a light, and the corrections of discipline are the way to life.
Proverbs 6:23 NIV

M A R C H   2 3

I recommend the HAT formula for decision-making at home. Hold off on all decisions if you are Hungry, Angry, or Tired.

Everyone should be quick to listen,
slow to speak and slow to become angry.
James 1:19,20 NIV

OCTOBER 10

Wives do not like to be taken for granted. So here is a simple little rule that should solve many husbands' problems: Do not let a day go by without praising your wife.

———————————

Praise her for the many fine things that she does. These good deeds of hers shall bring her honor and recognition from people of importance.
Proverbs 31:31 TLB

M A R C H   2 4

*G*od does not bring two people together just so they will have fun or will have someone to live with. He brings a man and a woman together to illustrate His love for His people.

Be devoted to one another in brotherly love.
Honor one another above yourselves.
Romans 12:10 NIV

O C T O B E R   9

*M*en, when was the last time you told your wife how special she is? When was the last time you took her in your arms and told her how happy you are that you chose her? Get to it!

_____

I am my beloved's, and his desire is toward me.
Song of Solomon 7:10 KJV

M A R C H   2 5

Children are not casual observers. They take in the whole scene, watching everybody, especially their parents. Like sponges, they soak it all in.

Be careful, and watch yourselves closely so that you do not forget the things your eyes have seen...teach them to your children and to their children after them.
Deuteronomy 4:9 NIV

OCTOBER 8

*T*here is no area in which God's resurrection power needs to be more graphically demonstrated than in marriage.

Now glory be to God who by his mighty power at work within us is able to do far more than we would ever dare to ask or even dream of—infinitely beyond our highest prayers, desires, thoughts, or hopes.
Ephesians 3:20 TLB

M A R C H   2 6

*W*aiting for an answer from God is hard. I don't know how long you will have to wait. All I know is that God's grace can strengthen you for as long as it takes.

I believe that I shall see the goodness of the Lord in the land of the living. Wait for the Lord; be strong, and let your heart take courage; wait for the Lord.
Psalm 27:13,14 NRSV

O C T O B E R   7

A man is no fool who uses biblical criteria in choosing a wife rather than secular standards.

_____

Charm is deceptive, and beauty is fleeting; but a woman who fears the Lord is to be praised.
Proverbs 31:30 NIV

M A R C H   2 7

*R*eal men hurt for others. They are involved in the community, making a difference for the have-nots of this world.

Since you have been chosen by God who has given you this new kind of life, and because of his deep love and concern for you, you should practice tenderhearted mercy and kindness to others.
Colossians 3:12 NRSV

O C T O B E R   6

In God's structure for marriage, the buck stops with the husband. He may not be the one doing the wrong, but he is responsible to keep things right.

_____

For the husband is the head of the wife
as Christ is the head of the church.
Ephesians 5:23 NIV

M A R C H 2 8

*I*f you want to keep a spark in your marriage, keep some special surprises in store for your spouse. Be listening for little hints; notice what makes your mate happy.

———————————————

Do not be interested only in your own life,
but be interested in the lives of others.
Philippians 2:4 NCV

O C T O B E R   5

*W*hen you consider the power of prayer,
it is no wonder Satan works overtime
to keep us off our knees.

---

*Therefore I tell you, whatever you ask for in prayer,
believe that you have received it, and it will be yours.*
Mark 11:24 NIV

M A R C H   2 9

*W*omen are to love their homes, not leave them.

Houses and wealth are inherited from parents,
but a prudent wife is from the Lord.
Proverbs 19:14 NIV

O C T O B E R   4

*D*o not wait to become perfect before
you begin teaching your children.
You will be waiting a long time.

Discipline your children while there is hope.
Proverbs 19:18 NRSV

M A R C H   3 0

When a family sits down to figure out their giving, their first question should be "How much do we love the Lord?" rather than "How much should we give?"

Give, and it shall be given unto you; good measure, pressed down, and shaken together, and running over.
Luke 6:38 KJV

O C T O B E R   3

*T*here is a difference between *essence* and *function*. Both marriage partners are equal in essence, but they differ in function.

In the Lord,...woman is not independent of man, nor is man independent of woman.
1 Corinthians 11:11 NIV

M A R C H   3 1

It is estimated that by the time he reaches age eighteen, a typical child will have spent twice as much time watching television as he has spent in school. Children would spend far less time in front of the TV if Mom and Dad were more involved in their lives.

Think constantly about these commandments....
Teach them to yur children and talk about them
when you are at home or out for a walk; at
bedtime and the first thing in the morning.
Deuteronomy 6:6,7 TLB

O C T O B E R   2

*Y*our manhood or your womanhood does not depend on your relationship with another person. It is who you are, uniquely created by God.

You formed my inward parts; You covered me in my mother's womb. I will praise You, for I am fearfully and wonderfully made.
Psalm 139:13,14 NKJV

A P R I L   1

*M*any husbands and wives work as a team to provide for the needs of their family. How beautiful it is when they bring that sense of teamwork home!

Make every effort to keep the unity of the Spirit through the bond of peace.
Ephesians 4:3 NIV

O C T O B E R   1

We live in a world where men, particularly in the minority community, are battered daily by an unjust society. But when a man comes home, things ought to be different. The home should be a haven from injustice.

The house of the righteous contains great treasure.
Proverbs 15:6 NIV

A P R I L   2

*W*hen God looks at a married couple, He does not see two people, but one. He sees two lives fused together to form one new life.

The two will become one flesh.
So they are no longer two, but one.
Mark 10:8 NIV

SEPTEMBER 30

*B*iblical submission is not slavery. It is placing oneself willingly under the authority of another. Jesus' relationship to His Father is our example.

———————————

And being found in appearance as a man,
he humbled himself and became obedient
to death—even death on a cross!
Philippians 2:8 NIV

A P R I L   3

*I*f you have not found your completeness in Christ, you will never find it in the secular marketplace.

_____

I have told you this so that my joy may be in you
and that your joy may be complete.
John 15:11 NIV

S E P T E M B E R   2 9

*C*hildren will not always do what they're told,
but they will do what they see!

Be an example to them of good deeds of every kind.
Let everything you do reflect your love of the truth.
Titus 2:7 TLB

A P R I L   4

A Christian couple has God on their side.
They do not need to give up or give in.

If God is for us, who can be against us?
Romans 8:31 NIV

SEPTEMBER 28

*T*here is nothing wrong with a woman making herself as attractive as she can. But God wants wives to arrange the *inside* so it is even more beautiful than the *outside!*

Be beautiful inside, in your hearts, with the
lasting charm of a gentle and quiet spirit
that is so precious to God.
1 Peter 3:4 TLB

A P R I L   5

*T*each your children a spiritual motivation for obedience. They should obey because it pleases the Lord.

————————————

Children, obey your parents in everything, for this is your acceptable duty in the Lord.
Colossians 3:20 NRSV

S E P T E M B E R   2 7

If your marriage is stuck on a merry-go-round and you are thinking about changing horses, talk to someone who has done that. You will find that the second horse is on the same merry-go-round as the first!

Agree with one another so that there may be no divisions among you and that you may be perfectly united in mind and thought.
1 Corinthians 1:10 NIV

A P R I L   6

The welfare of a wife is in her husband's hands. What an exciting opportunity he has to take care of a special woman!

_____

Husbands,...be considerate as you live with your wives, and treat them with respect.
1 Peter 3:7 NIV

S E P T E M B E R   2 6

A man should come home to give, not to get. He should seek to serve his wife and family, even when he is tired and hungry and has had a rough day at work.

_____

Remembering the words of the Lord Jesus, for he himself said, "It is more blessed to give than to receive."
Acts 20:35 NKJV

A P R I L   7

A woman's home should be her top priority. Once she determines what is necessary to make the home function as it should, and knows what she is inclined to do that will not interfere with her priorities, then she may decide what she is free to do outside the home.

_____

So whether we are at home or away,
we make it our aim to please him.
2 Corinthians 5:9 NRSV

S E P T E M B E R   2 5

Freedom is not being able to indulge all of your desires. That is slavery to the world. Real freedom is the ability to say, "I don't need any woman (or man) but the one God has given me."

I run in the path of your commands,
for you have set my heart free.
Psalm 119:32 NIV

A P R I L 8

A good marriage is the sum of a lot of little things.

Set me as a seal upon thine heart, as a seal
upon thine arm: for love is strong as death.
Song of Solomon 8:6 KJV

SEPTEMBER 24

The world has given us a poor definition of freedom. Walking the way of this world is slavery that just feels like freedom for a little while.

Then you will know the truth, and the truth will set you free.
John 8:32 NIV

A P R I L   9

When my wife Lois and I began dating, she told me of her commitment to Jesus Christ and her intention to remain pure until she was married. I respected her so much for that.

Whatever is true, whatever is noble, whatever is right, whatever is pure, whatever is lovely, whatever is admirable—if anything is excellent or praiseworthy—think about such things.
Philippians 4:8 NIV

S E P T E M B E R   2 3

*W*hat the church and the world around us need today is men who will stand up and say without apology, "You do whatever you want. But as for this leader and his family, we will serve the Lord!"

Love the Lord and follow his plan for your lives.
Cling to him and serve him enthusiastically.
Joshua 22:5 TLB

APRIL 10

*T*he godly man is a man of compassion and mercy. He is a protector of the helpless.

———————————————

I rescued the poor who cried for help, and
the fatherless who had none to assist him....
I was a father to the needy.
Job 29:12,16 NIV

SEPTEMBER 22

*I*s there anything around your house that could draw you or your family away from the Lord? If so, do whatever God tells you to do to correct it.

And when you draw close to God, God will draw close to you.... Let your hearts be filled with God alone to make them pure and true to him.
James 4:8 TLB

A P R I L   1 1

*W*hen a woman feels loved, she has no problem loving. When a woman feels cared for, she has no problem caring.

Husbands, love your wives, just as Christ loved the church and gave himself up for her.
Ephesians 5:25 NRSV

SEPTEMBER 21

*C*onflicts in marriage are normal, natural, and to be expected. They do not have to put out the flame.

Bear with each other and forgive whatever grievances you may have against one another. Forgive as the Lord forgave you.
Colossians 3:13 NIV

A P R I L   1 2

*G*ive your children a home—not so they can stay home—but so they will know how to live when they leave home.

_____

Train a child in the way he should go, and when he is old he will not turn from it.
Proverbs 22:6 NIV

S E P T E M B E R   2 0

A woman does not marry a paycheck, she marries a man. She wants her husband's love and attention, not his business card.

I am my beloved's, and his desire is toward me.
Song of Solomon 7:10 TLB

A P R I L   1 3

*W*hat makes the "ideal wife" of Proverbs so rare is that everything she does is for the enhancement of her home.

———————————

Who can find a virtuous woman?
for her price is far above rubies.
Proverbs 31:10 KJV

S E P T E M B E R   1 9

*P*arents cannot please their children all of the time. If they do, the children are being allowed to play a decision-making role that only the parents should fill!

_____

For the Lord reproves the one he loves,
as a father the son in whom he delights.
Proverbs 3:12 NRSV

A P R I L   1 4

Do you want to really wow your wife? Deliberately give up an activity or event that she knows means a lot to you. When she asks why, just say, "Yes, I was supposed to do that. But you know, I would just rather be with you."

How delightful is your love....
How much more pleasing is your love.
Song of Songs 4:10 NIV

S E P T E M B E R   1 8

*G*od's Word says husbands need to know their wives. They need to understand what makes them tick. It will pay huge dividends.

———————————————

You husbands should live with your wives in an understanding way.... But show them respect.... Do this so that nothing will stop your prayers.
1 Peter 3:7 NCV

A P R I L   1 5

People who are committed to Jesus Christ have a goal in life that far surpasses any other goal. That goal is to bring glory to God.

———————————————

To the only wise God be glory forever through Jesus Christ!
Romans 16:27 NIV

S E P T E M B E R   1 7

The first step in relighting the flame in a marriage is deciding to do it. Rekindling starts with a decision of the will, not a feeling in the stomach.

―――――――――――――

We pray that with his power God will help you do the good things you want and perform the works that come from your faith.
2 Thessalonians 1:11 NCV

A P R I L   1 6

*S*ingle Christian women can help single Christian men grow to maturity by holding to high personal standards. They may remind the men that they are responsible not only for their own holiness in body and spirit, but also for the holiness of any woman they date.

It is God's will that you should be sanctified: that you should avoid sexual immorality; that each of you should learn to control his own body in a way that is holy and honorable.
1 Thessalonians 4:3,4 NIV

S E P T E M B E R   1 6

*Y*ou may trip and stumble a thousand times on your journey with your children. But if they know you love the Lord and love them and are doing the best you can, it will make up for a lot of mistakes.

———————————

Above all, love each other deeply, because
love covers over a multitude of sins.
1 Peter 4:8 NIV

A P R I L   1 7

A parent's job in discipline is to "adjust" his child's will without breaking his spirit.

Fathers, do not provoke your children,
or they may lose heart.
Colossians 3:21 NRSV

S E P T E M B E R   1 5

*H*usbands, when you said "I do," nobody forced you to say that. *You* made the commitment—now stick with it!

_____

Be strong in the Lord, and in
the power of his might.
Ephesians 6:10

A P R I L   1 8

$\mathcal{I}$f you are living any old kind of life, and if you have not noticed God's discipline in your life, maybe you had better check the name on your "new birth" certificate!

If anyone is in Christ, he is a new creation; the old has gone, the new has come!
2 Corinthians 5:17 NIV

S E P T E M B E R   1 4

Prayer is not the only thing you need to do. It is just the *first* thing you need to do.

But I, O Lord, cry out to you; in the morning my prayer comes before you.
Psalm 88:13 NRSV

A P R I L   1 9

God has absolute jurisdiction over His children.

---

*The same Lord is Lord of all and richly
blesses all who call on him.*
Romans 10:12 NIV

S E P T E M B E R   1 3

$\mathcal{I}$f you have to think back to the early days of your relationship to remember having good times together, begin to work now to make *these* days the "good old days."

He who began a good work in you will carry it on to completion until the day of Christ Jesus.
Philippians 1:6 NIV

A P R I L   2 0

*I*n society today, we have a huge percentage of women in the work force. Our homes are feeling the effect of this; a home is not necessarily improved by outside activities.

A wife of noble character who can find?...
She watches over the affairs of her household.
Proverbs 31:10,27 NIV

S E P T E M B E R   1 2

*P*ut those forgotten little kindnesses back into your marriage. Open the car door for her, offer her your hand. It will feel great, and some brother who is watching you across the church parking lot will get the same idea!
Then you will have two winners!

_____

Love is kind.
1 Corinthians 13:4 NIV

A P R I L   2 9

*W*ives, when God tells you to submit to your husbands, He is not asking you to do anything that He did not ask Jesus to do for you!

Your attitude should be the kind that was shown us by Jesus Christ, who, though he was God, did not demand and cling to his rights as God.
Philippians 2:5,6 TLB

S E P T E M B E R   3

$\mathcal{M}$en, take leadership of your homes.
Be men of biblical love and authority.

_____

I walk in the way of righteousness,
along the paths of justice.
Proverbs 8:20 NIV

A P R I L   3 0

*W*hen it comes to teaching children the Word of God and how to live, the church is only a helper for the home, not a replacement.

And these words which I command you today shall be in your heart. You shall teach them diligently to your children.
Deuteronomy 6:6, 7 NKJV

SEPTEMBER 2

*W*ives, honor your husbands' desire to be leaders by giving them the support they need in order to be what God has called them to be.

Wives, submit to your husbands as to the Lord.
Ephesians 5:22 NIV

M A Y 1

A Christian home is not just a place where Christians live. It is a home where the authority of Jesus Christ rules the members of that household.

———————————————

You are...members of the household of God, built upon the foundation of the apostles and prophets, with Christ Jesus himself as the cornerstone.
Ephesians 2:19.20 NRSV

S E P T E M B E R   1

*R*emember when your grandfather or grandmother used to talk about right and wrong? They were passing down a divine heritage to you, to be passed on to your children.

_____

May his miracles have a deep and permanent effect upon your lives! Tell your children and your grandchildren about the glorious miracles he did. Deuteronomy 4:9. TLB

M A Y   2

Is your wife or your husband your best friend? Is your mate the person with whom you share your total being? If not, start the process today!

This is my lover, this my friend.
Song of Songs 5:16 NIV

A U G U S T   3 1

*W*hen it comes to nurturing your marriage,
begin with the little things.

_____

*Let us love, not in word or speech,
but in truth and action.*
1 John 3:18 NRSV

M A Y   3

When others say they cannot make it in their marriages or in their families, God wants you to step up and witness to His power to hold relationships together.

But he said to me, "My grace is sufficient for you, for power is made perfect in weakness." So, I will boast all the more gladly of my weaknesses, so that the power of Christ may dwell in me.
2 Corinthians 12:9 NRSV

A U G U S T   3 0

*A*nything a woman does outside her home is a bonus. That does not mean she cannot have a career, but the home is to be her priority.

———————————————

To be self-controlled and pure, to be busy at home, to be kind, and to be subject to their husbands, so that no one will malign the word of God.
Titus 2:5 NIV

M A Y   4

*E*verybody wants to be graded on the curve,
because then nobody looks too bad. But God
wants to use your family to break the curve,
to show how families are supposed to work.

Be imitators of God, therefore, as dearly loved children.
Ephesians 5:1 NIV

AUGUST 29

$\mathcal{T}$here is nothing wrong with wanting nice things. There is everything wrong with wanting nice things at the expense of biblical priorities in the home.

_____

For where your treasure is, there your heart will be also.
Matthew 6:21 NKJV

M A Y   5

*M*any married couples are fighting *against* each other rather than *for* each other. Let's get on the same team and fight the good fight of faith together.

———————————

Fight the good fight of the faith. Take hold of the eternal life to which you were called when you made your good confession in the presence of many witnesses.
1 Timothy 6:12 NIV

A U G U S T   2 8

*G*od's desire is always to keep a marriage together. Repentance and forgiveness are the best way to go.

_____

Bear with each other and forgive whatever grievances you may have against one another. Forgive as the Lord forgave you.
Colossians 3:13 NIV

M A Y 6

We all want to get back to paradise. But what will it take to get there? It will take men who have the courage to run their homes according to the Boss's instructions. Your Boss, men, is God!

Now I want you to realize that the head of every man is Christ, and the head of the woman is man, and the head of Christ is God.
1 Corinthians 11:3 NIV

AUGUST 27

*P*ut those forgotten little kindnesses back into your marriage. Open the car door for her, offer her your hand. It will feel great, and some brother who is watching you across the church parking lot will get the same idea!
Then you will have two winners!

Love is kind.
1 Corinthians 13:4 NIV

A P R I L   2 9

Wives, when God tells you to submit to your husbands, He is not asking you to do anything that He did not ask Jesus to do for you!

———————————

Your attitude should be the kind that was shown us by Jesus Christ, who, though he was God, did not demand and cling to his rights as God.
Philippians 2:5,6 TLB

S E P T E M B E R   3

*M*en, take leadership of your homes.
Be men of biblical love and authority.

I walk in the way of righteousness,
along the paths of justice.
Proverbs 8:20 *NIV*

A P R I L   3 0

*W*hen it comes to teaching children the Word of God and how to live, the church is only a helper for the home, not a replacement.

———————————————

And these words which I command you today shall be in your heart. You shall teach them diligently to your children.
Deuteronomy 6:6,7 NKJV

S E P T E M B E R   2

*W*ives, honor your husbands' desire to be leaders by giving them the support they need in order to be what God has called them to be.

Wives, submit to your husbands as to the Lord.
Ephesians 5:22 NIV

M A Y 1

A Christian home is not just a place where Christians live. It is a home where the authority of Jesus Christ rules the members of that household.

———————————

You are...members of the household of God, built upon the foundation of the apostles and prophets, with Christ Jesus himself as the cornerstone.
Ephesians 2:19.20 NRSV

S E P T E M B E R   1

$\mathcal{R}$emember when your grandfather or grandmother used to talk about right and wrong? They were passing down a divine heritage to you, to be passed on to your children.

———————————————

May his miracles have a deep and permanent effect upon your lives! Tell your children and your grandchildren about the glorious miracles he did. Deuteronomy 4:9. TLB

M A Y   2

Is your wife or your husband your best friend? Is your mate the person with whom you share your total being? If not, start the process today!

_____

This is my lover, this my friend.
Song of Songs 5:16 NIV

A U G U S T   3 1

*W*hen it comes to nurturing your marriage, begin with the little things.

---

*Let us love, not in word or speech,
but in truth and action.*
1 John 3:18 NRSV

M A Y   3

When others say they cannot make it in their marriages or in their families, God wants you to step up and witness to His power to hold relationships together.

But he said to me, "My grace is sufficient for you, for power is made perfect in weakness." So, I will boast all the more gladly of my weaknesses, so that the power of Christ may dwell in me.
2 Corinthians 12:9 NRSV

A U G U S T   3 0

*A*nything a woman does outside her home is a bonus. That does not mean she cannot have a career, but the home is to be her priority.

———————————————

To be self-controlled and pure, to be busy at home, to be kind, and to be subject to their husbands, so that no one will malign the word of God.
Titus 2:5 NIV

M A Y 4

*E*verybody wants to be graded on the curve, because then nobody looks too bad. But God wants to use your family to break the curve, to show how families are supposed to work.

———————————

Be imitators of God, therefore, as dearly loved children.
Ephesians 5:1 NIV

A U G U S T   2 9

There is nothing wrong with wanting nice things. There is everything wrong with wanting nice things at the expense of biblical priorities in the home.

———————

For where your treasure is, there your heart will be also.
Matthew 6:21 NKJV

M A Y   5

$\mathcal{M}$any married couples are fighting *against* each other rather than *for* each other. Let's get on the same team and fight the good fight of faith together.

Fight the good fight of the faith. Take hold of the eternal life to which you were called when you made your good confession in the presence of many witnesses.
1 Timothy 6:12 NIV

A U G U S T   2 8

$\mathcal{G}$od's desire is always to keep a marriage together. Repentance and forgiveness are the best way to go.

_____

Bear with each other and forgive whatever grievances you may have against one another. Forgive as the Lord forgave you.
Colossians 3:13 NIV

M A Y   6

We all want to get back to paradise. But what will it take to get there? It will take men who have the courage to run their homes according to the Boss's instructions. Your Boss, men, is God!

———————————

Now I want you to realize that the head of every man is Christ, and the head of the woman is man, and the head of Christ is God.
1 Corinthians 11:3 NIV

A U G U S T   2 7

On the busiest, most intense, most heavily
scheduled day of His life, Jesus took
the time to pray.

Then Jesus brought them to a garden grove,
Gethsemane, and told them to sit down and
wait while he went on ahead to pray.
Matthew 26:36 TLB

M A Y 7

$\mathcal{H}$ow do a father and mother fight for their children? They get down on their knees together.

For our struggle is not against flesh and blood, but against the rulers, against the authorities, against the powers of this dark world and against the spiritual forces of evil in the heavenly realms.
Ephesians 6:12 NIV

AUGUST 26

*C*hristian marriage is designed
to make God look good!

But you are a chosen people, a royal priesthood,
a holy nation, a people belonging to God, that
you may declare the praises of him who called
you out of darkness into his wonderful light.
1 Peter 2:9 NIV

M A Y   8

The scope of a wife's submission to her husband and of children's obedience to their parents is this: no more than what is "fitting in the Lord."

Wives, submit to your husbands, as is fitting in the Lord.... Children, obey your parents in everything, for this pleases the Lord.
Colossians 3:18,20 NIV

AUGUST 25

If you are married, do not look for a way out.
If you are single, do not become obsessed
with getting married.

I have learned to be content with whatever I have.
Philippians 4:11 NRSV

M A Y   9

Children do not have to agree with their parents to be able to honor and to obey them in the Lord.

Children, obey your parents in the Lord, for this is right.
Ephesians 6:1 NRSV

A U G U S T   2 4

My wife and I have pledged to never even
mention the words "separation" or "divorce."
There is no terminology in our house
for any of that.

Finally, brothers, whatever is true, whatever is noble,
whatever is right, whatever is pure, whatever is lovely,
whatever is admirable—if anything is excellent or
praiseworthy—think about such things.
Philippians 4:8 NIV

M A Y   1 0

How we relate to our children is formative. It has a great deal to do with how they will turn out.

_____

The righteous man leads a blameless life;
blessed are his children after him.
Proverbs 20:7 NIV

AUGUST 23

You do not need an extensive education to be wise. The old folks called wisdom common sense.

Let the wise listen and add to their learning, and let the discerning get guidance.... The fear of the Lord is the beginning of knowledge.
Proverbs 1:5,7 NIV

M A Y   1 1

To love our mates the way God wants us to love them requires the work of the Holy Spirit. That is why the filling of the Spirit and the supernatural life are essential to a successful marriage.

Guard the good treasure entrusted to you, with the help of the Holy Spirit living in us.
2 Timothy 1:14 NRSV

A U G U S T   2 2

When it comes to making your marriage work, stop listening to your friends and neighbors and the television and start listening to God.

———————

How does a man become wise? The first step is to trust and reverence the Lord!
Proverbs 1:7 TLB

M A Y 1 2

*H*ow a man treats his wife is a reflection of what he thinks about God.

Your attitude should be the same as that of Christ Jesus.
Philippians 2:5 NIV

AUGUST 21

When was the last time you wrote your spouse a love letter? Get a stamp and get busy!

_____

I am my lover's and my lover is mine.
Song of Solomon 6:3 NIV

M A Y 1 3

Satan's strategy of going after our marriages and families is nothing new. He didn't show up in the Garden of Eden until Adam was married!

———————————————

Now the serpent was more crafty than any of the wild animals the Lord God had made.
Genesis 3:1 NIV

A U G U S T   2 0

The world is trying to influence us. But we can put a stop to it right in our homes by knowing what is going on in our families.

For all that is in the world...comes not from the Father but from the world.
1 John 2:16 NRSV

M A Y   1 4

*T*o become all you were created to be, you must learn to accept the strength your mate offers.

———————————

Iron sharpens iron, and one person sharpens...another.
Proverbs 27:17 NRSV

A U G U S T   1 9

$\mathcal{M}$en can do without love, but they cannot function without respect.

_____

And the wife must respect her husband.
Ephesians 5:33 NIV

MAY 15

A man armed with biblical love will sacrifice anything that interferes with his calling as a husband and father. We men owe nothing less to our families and to God.

Let love and faithfulness never leave you;...
write them on the tablet of your heart.
Proverbs 3:3 NIV

AUGUST 18

*I*f God gives you an opportunity to climb the ladder of success, climb it. But not at the expense of your home.

As long as he sought the Lord, God gave him success.
2 Chronicles 26:5 NIV

M A Y   1 6

*A*lmost any relationship problem can be solved if both parties will think about the other person and ask, "What have I done for you lately?"

We know love by this, that he laid down his life for us—and we ought to lay down our lives for one another.
1 John 3:16 NRSV

AUGUST 17

*O*lder women can have a wonderful ministry by teaching younger women how to love their husbands.

_____

Likewise, teach the older women to be reverent in the way they live...then they can train the younger women to love their husbands and children.
Titus 2:3,4 NIV

M A Y   1 7

Husband, surprise your wife by calling her from work for no reason other than to say, "I was sitting here thinking about you, and I can't get you off my mind. I just wanted to hear your voice."

———————————

Let me see your face, Let me hear your voice;
For your voice is sweet, and your face is lovely.
Song of Solomon 2:14 NKJV

AUGUST 16

*T*he Christian life is not a life of ease. It is composed of many acts of the will whereby we obey God for the glory of God.

So whether you eat or drink or whatever
you do, do it all for the glory of God.
1 Corinthians 10:31 *NIV*

M A Y   1 8

*A*s Christians our job is to retain the glory of God even though society does not reflect it.

In him we were also chosen,...in order that we, who were the first to hope in Christ, might be for the praise of his glory.
Ephesians 1:11,12 NIV

A U G U S T   1 5

*A*gape love is not discussion love. It is more than mere words that sound good. Agape love is always *demonstrated* love.

But God demonstrates his own love for us in this: While we were still sinners, Christ died for us.
Romans 5:8 NIV

M A Y   1 9

Parents are unique in their children's lives because of their God-given authority to correct their children.

Children, obey your parents; this is the right thing to do because God has placed them in authority over you.
Ephesians 6:1 TLB

AUGUST 14

A husband's love for his wife is measured by actions, not by vocabulary. It is measured by what he does for her, not by what he says.

Husbands ought to love their wives as their own bodies. He who loves his wife loves himself. After all, no one ever hated his own body, but he feeds and cares for it, just as Christ does the church.
Eph. 5:28,29 NIV

M A Y   2 0

A godly woman who dedicates herself to her husband and children makes an investment more worthwhile than anything Wall Street has to offer.

Her children arise and call her blessed; her husband also, and he praises her: "Many women do noble things, but you surpass them all.
Proverbs 31:28,29 NIV

A U G U S T   1 3

*I*t is easy to leave your spouse and find someone else who has not had to live with you yet. Stick by your vows even when it is tough.

_____

Rejoice in the wife of your youth....
Let her love alone fill you with delight.
Proverbs 5:18,19 TLB

M A Y   2 1

The church needs to fight the world for the family.
Parents need to fight the enemy for their children.
Married people need to fight for their marriage.
Family is worth fighting for!

———————————

*Stand firm then, with the belt of truth buckled around
your waist, with the breastplate of righteousness in place.*
Ephesians 6:14 NIV

A U G U S T   1 2

*H*onoring your father and mother may take different forms at different stages in your life. But the principle always remains in effect.

———————————————

Honor your father and your mother, as the Lord your God has commanded you, so that you may live long and that it may go well with you.
Deuteronomy 5:16 NIV

MAY 22

The ultimate authority for how a man should treat his wife is divine authority. It makes no difference what others say.

_____

And you have been given fullness in Christ, who is the head over every power and authority.
Colossians 2:10 NIV

AUGUST 11

One of the ways a husband loves his wife is by learning to read her so he knows how she feels and what she wants.

_____

Counsel in another's heart is like deep water,
but a discerning person will draw it up.
Proverbs 20:5 REB

M A Y   2 3

*W*hen children do not obey their parents immediately, they start down a road on which disobedience becomes progressively easier, until the time comes to pay a big price.

For these commands are a lamp, this teaching is a light, and the corrections of discipline are the way to life.
Proverbs 6:23 NIV

A U G U S T   1 0

A vital part of a husband's job is to make his wife feel good about herself.

You have stolen my heart, my sister, my bride.
Song of Solomon 4:9 NIV

M A Y   2 4

$\mathcal{I}$n the first marriage, God gave away the bride.
When you stood at the altar and repeated
your vows, God also ordained your union.

———————————

What therefore God hath joined together,
let not man put asunder.
Mark 10:9 KJV

A U G U S T   9

The world tells single people, "It's your body. Do whatever you want with it." But God says, "Bad information! You belong to Me. And I have better plans for you."

You were bought at a price. Therefore honor God with your body.
1 Corinthians 6:20 NIV

M A Y   2 5

The acid test showing whether or not you are filled with the Holy Spirit is how you live at home.

_____

But the fruit of the Spirit is love, joy, peace, patience, kindness, goodness, faithfulness, gentleness and self-control.
Galatians 5:22,23 NIV

A U G U S T   8

*W*e need to love our mates in such a self-giving way that we do not demand anything in return. Whatever we get back is a bonus.

———————————————

Love must be sincere.... Cling to what is good.
Romans 12:9 NIV

M A Y   2 6

In Titus 2, Paul is not necessarily telling women to stay home. He is telling them to love their homes. Anything that interferes with this needs to be dealt with and removed.

Younger women may learn to love their husbands and their children, to be sensible and chaste, home-lovers, kind-hearted and willing to adapt themselves to their husbands—a good advertisement for the Christian faith.
Titus 2:4 PHILLIPS

AUGUST 7

Do not say to your mate, "All right, I'll do this, but only if you do that." Jesus did not say that to us when it came to salvation. Let's not put that load on our mates.

As the Father has loved me, so have I loved you.
Now remain in my love.
John 15:9 NIV

M A Y   2 7

$\mathcal{A}$ man benefits when he uses the expertise of his wife to help him accomplish God's calling.

A capable wife who can find? She
is far more precious than jewels.
Proverbs 31:10 NRSV

AUGUST 6

*T*he best and most effective thing we can ever do for our children is to pray for them every day.

In the morning, O Lord, you hear my voice;
in the morning I lay my requests before you
and wait in expectation.
Psalm 5:3 NIV

M A Y   2 8

The more mature you get, the more you understand that you cannot manage your home or your life without God's help.

If any of you lacks wisdom, he should ask God, who gives generously to all without finding fault, and it will be given to him.
James 1:5 NIV

AUGUST 5

$\mathcal{M}$en, your wife is your equal. You are the head of the home, but she is your equal in essence and in value to the Lord. Treat her as an equal.

So God created man in his own image, in the image of God he created him; male and female he created them.
Genesis 1:27 NIV

MAY 29

$\mathcal{H}$usband, set the direction for your home, or your wife will be forced to do it for you. That will not fulfill her—it is not what God intended her to do.

Each of you, however, should love his wife as himself, and a wife should respect her husband.
Ephesians 5:33 NRSV

AUGUST 4

The level of communication a husband experiences with God is related to his willingness to communicate with his wife in a sensitive and loving way.

You married men should live considerately with your wives, with an intelligent recognition of the marriage relation, honoring the woman.
1 Peter 3:7 AMP

M A Y   3 0

A confused man creates a confused family,
but a clear-minded man provides stability.

In you, O Lord, I have taken refuge;
let me never be put to shame.
Psalm 71:1 NIV

AUGUST 3

*A*ny young man who wants to date my daughter has to come and meet with me first. If he doesn't respect me enough as a father to meet me, he probably will not respect my daughter enough to treat her right either.

Live as those who are free to do only God's will at all times. Show respect for everyone.
1 Peter 2:16,17 TLB

MAY 31

*A*dam was to be God's assistant on earth while Eve was to come alongside Adam to be his assistant.

Then the Lord God said, "It is not good that the man should be alone; I will make him a helper as his partner."
Genesis 2:18 NRSV

A U G U S T   2

*M*en, you have authority in your homes, no question about it. But your authority is limited to what you are *supposed* to do, not to whatever you want to do.

———————————————

Now I want you to realize that the head of every man is Christ, and the head of the woman is man, and the head of Christ is God.
1 Corinthians 11:3 NIV

J U N E   1

The two qualities a woman should look for in a husband are submission to God and a willingness to work.

Whatever your task, put yourselves into it, as done for the Lord and not for your masters.
Colossians 3:23 NRSV

A U G U S T   1

$\mathcal{H}$usbands have to place themselves under God's authority in order to make their authority in the family legitimate.

———————————————

For the husband is the head of the wife as Christ is the head of the church, his body, of which he is the Savior.
Ephesians 5:23 NIV

J U N E   2

$\mathcal{H}$ow a man responds to the authority of God in his life determines how his wife will fare in their marriage.

Agree with God, and be at peace;
in this way good will come to you.
Job 22:21 NRSV

J U L Y   3 1

*T*here is no reason to divorce for "irreconcilable differences." Whenever you have two sinners in the same house, you will be irreconcilable about something!

To the married I give this command (not I, but the Lord): A wife must not separate from her husband. But if she does, she must remain unmarried or else be reconciled to her husband. And a husband must not divorce his wife.
1 Corinthians 7:10,11 NIV

J U N E   3

$\mathcal{T}$he world says "the more children you have, the poorer you are." The Bible says "the more children you have, the richer you are."

_____

Sons are a heritage from the Lord,
children a reward from him.
Psalm 127:3 NIV

J U L Y   3 0

Kids, the promise that goes with obedience or lack of obedience to your parents could determine your whole future.

Honor your father and your mother, so that you may live long in the land the Lord your God is giving you.
Exodus 20:12 NIV

J U N E   4

*I*f your children need help in obeying, help them! Help them by correcting them just as God corrects us. He says, "If I did not discipline you, you would belong to the neighbor. You would not be my child."

The Lord disciplines those he loves, and he punishes everyone he accepts as a son.
Hebrews 12:6 NIV

J U L Y   2 9

Fathers need to be home long enough to know what their children are watching on TV, and to turn it off if necessary. If fathers are not there, they will lose the leadership of the home.

And fathers...bring them up in the discipline
and instruction of the Lord.
Ephesians 6:4 NRSV

J U N E   5

*M*an was created to be the chief manager of God's creation.

Then God said, "Let us make humankind in our image, according to our likeness; and let them have dominion over the fish of the sea, and over the birds of the air, and over the cattle, and over all the wild animals of the earth, and over every creeping thing that creeps upon the earth."

Genesis 1:26 NRSV

J U L Y   2 8

The noble woman of Proverbs 31 chose work that complemented rather than contradicted her home.

She considers a field and buys it; out of her earnings she plants a vineyard.
Proverbs 31:16 NIV

J U N E   6

*B*iblical love is sacrificial, but we do not know what sacrifice means anymore.

Therefore, I urge you, brothers, in view of God's mercy, to offer your bodies as living sacrifices, holy and pleasing to God—this is your spiritual act of worship.
Romans 12:1 NIV

J U L Y   2 7

*E*ver since God had to go looking for Adam, the challenge for men has been to stay put and face their responsibilities instead of taking off.

Love...always perseveres.
1 Corinthians 13:6,7 NIV

God asks a man to give up the closest ties he has, to his parents, because one of a woman's greatest needs in marriage is for security.

———————————————

Enjoy life with your wife, whom you love, all the days of this...life that God has given you under the sun.
Ecclesiastes 9:9 NIV

J U L Y   2 6

The first thing that God's people have been called to do is to pray.

_____

I urge, then, first of all, that requests, prayers, intercession and thanksgiving be made for everyone.
1 Timothy 2:1 NIV

JUNE 8

A biblical lover is one who initiates. God so loved that He *gave*. He took the first step.

For God so loved the world, that he gave his only begotten Son, that whosoever believeth in him should not perish, but have everlasting life.
John 3:16 KJV

JULY 25

$\mathcal{M}$en, how you treat your wives is very important to God. Treating them with love and respect rates high with Him.

A new command I give you: Love one another.
As I have loved you, so you must love one another.
John 13:34 NIV

J U N E   9

*I*n marriage money needs to be considered "ours" rather than "mine" and "yours," or you are headed for problems. Sit down together and prepare a budget you can both agree on.

_____

For the love of money is a root of all kinds of evil. Some people, eager for money, have wandered from the faith.
1 Timothy 6:10 NIV

J U L Y   2 4

$\mathcal{D}$o all you can to encourage and support every man in the minority community who is a godly man and a leader in his family!

_____

You, my brothers, were called to be free....
Serve one another in love.
Galatians 5:13 NIV

J U N E   1 0

*T*ell your children what to believe.
If you don't, someone else will.

---

*Teach a child to choose the right path, and
when he is older, he will remain upon it.*
Proverbs 22:6 *TLB*

JULY 23

A Christian marriage partner has a frame of
reference totally different from the world's values.
Instead of saying, "This is what you should
do for me," a Christian mate says,
"Honey, what are your needs?"

But the fruit of the Spirit is...gentleness.
Galatians 5:22,23 NIV

J U N E   1 1

The apostle Paul encouraged singleness as the more desirable lifestyle in light of the larger goal of serving Christ with maximum effectiveness.

_____

I would like you to be free from concern.
An unmarried man is concerned about the
Lord's affairs—how he can please the Lord.
1 Corinthians 7:32 NIV

J U L Y   2 2

Our communities need men who have the stamina and the ability to stand up and take back the leadership of their homes.

You...are from God and have overcome them, because the one who is in you is greater than the one who is in the world.
1 John 4:4 NIV

J U N E   1 2

$\mathcal{T}$he Rambo or Dirty Harry approach does not work in a marriage. In real life, a husband needs to be sensitive and to care about those he leads.

And be kind to one another, tenderhearted, forgiving one another, just as God in Christ also forgave you.
Ephesians 4:32 NKJV

J U L Y   2 1

When was the last time you took your mate by the hand and said, "Let's go for a walk"? Do it today!

The winter is past; the rains are over and gone. Flowers appear on the earth; the season of singing has come, the cooing of doves is heard in our land.... Arise, come, my darling; my beautiful one, come with me.
Song of Songs 2:11-13 NIV

J U N E   1 3

*W*hen a Christian wife and mother says, "I have to have work to be fulfilled," she is really saying, "I need a change in my outward circumstances to be complete." That is shaky ground for any Christian.

_____

I have learned the secret of being content in any and every situation.... I can do everything through him who gives me strength.
Philippians 4:12,13 NIV

J U L Y   2 0

I have never heard so much "my money, your money" talk between husbands and wives as I am hearing today. But the Bible makes it clear that "the two shall become one flesh." And that means one in every way.

And the two will become one flesh.
Ephesians 5:31 NIV

J U N E   1 4

*M*arriage is God's idea. That is why it is a divine covenant rather than a human agreement.

He ordained his covenant forever—holy and awesome is his name.
Psalm 111:9 NIV

J U L Y   1 9

We need to distinguish the *purpose* of marriage from its *benefits.* The purpose of Christian marriage is to serve as an illustration of Christ and the church. The benefits of marriage are love, security, etc.

———————————

And when we obey him, every path he guides us on is fragrant with his lovingkindness and his truth.
Psalm 25:10 TLB

J U N E   1 5

I love my dad. He worked so hard and did without so much to raise us. Recently he told me, "When I see what you're doing in the ministry, how you love Christ, how you're raising your children, I know that the sacrifice was all worth it."

I am the good shepherd; I know my sheep and my sheep know me—just as the Father knows me and I know the Father—and I lay down my life for the sheep.
John 10:12-15 NIV

JULY 18

*I*n the end, the truth about love is simple but biblical: Talk is cheap. Love *is* as love *does*.

Live a life of love, just as Christ loved us and gave himself up for us as a fragrant offering and sacrifice to God.
Ephesians 5:2 NIV

J U N E   1 6

*G*entlemen, you never know what a gentle touch will do for a woman.

―――――――――

Kiss me again and again, for your love is sweeter than wine.
Song of Solomon 1:2 TLB

J U L Y   1 7

If you are married and nothing has changed in your agenda, you had better look again. When you get married, your life is supposed to change.

Be made new in the attitude of your minds;
and...put on the new self, created to be like
God in true righteousness and holiness.
Ephesians 4:22-24 NIV

J U N E   1 7

$\mathcal{I}$f you leave a problem with God, it will be solved right the first time. But if you insist on fixing it your own way, your solution will fail and you will have to start over God's way.

Trust in the Lord with all your heart, and lean not on your own understanding; in all your ways acknowledge Him, and He shall direct your paths.
Proverbs 3:5,6 NKJV

JULY 16

*W*hen husbands are critical of their wives, I say, "OK, she has a problem. What is your strategy for helping her to overcome it?" They usually do not have one. Don't criticize, strategize!

Love...believes all things, hopes all things.
1 Corinthians 13:7 NKJV

JUNE 18

What a blessing it is when a father can say to his family, "Follow me as I follow the Lord."

He did what was right in the eyes of the Lord, just as his father...had done.
2 Chronicles 26:4 NIV

J U L Y   1 5

Fathers, do not neglect the spiritual rearing of your children. That is your responsibility.

---

*Fathers, do not exasperate your children;
instead, bring them up in the training
and instruction of the Lord.*
Ephesians 6:4 NIV

J U N E   1 9

The Bible says that when you meet an older woman, you are to treat her like your mother.

But speak...to older women as mothers, to younger women as sisters—with absolute purity.
1 Timothy 5:1,2 NRSV

J U L Y   1 4

$\mathscr{W}$hen you are faithful to your marriage under God, you set your children up for some terrific blessings.

———————————

A faithful man will be richly blessed.
Proverbs 28:20 NIV

JUNE 20

*T*he Bible says that when you meet an older man, you are to treat him like your father.

Do not speak harshly to an older man, but speak to him as to a father.
1 Timothy 5:1 NRSV

J U L Y   1 3

*G*od created marriage for three purposes—procreation, dominion, and self-fulfillment. He has higher plans for your marriage than your happiness alone.

God blessed them and said to them, "Be fruitful and increase in number; fill the earth and subdue it. Rule over the fish of the sea and the birds of the air and over every living creature that moves on the ground."
Genesis 1:28 NIV

JUNE 21

The husband-wife relationship is more important than the parent-child relationship. You are preparing your children to leave someday. But remember, your mate will be there for the long haul.

Honor your marriage and its vows, and be pure.
Hebrews 13:4 TLB

J U L Y   1 2

The Bible consistently holds a couple's desire for children in the highest regard.

Children are a gift from God; they are his reward....
Happy is the man who has his quiver full of them.
Psalm 127:3,5 TLB

JUNE 22

*T*he husband is responsible for the condition of his home. In the garden, God did not go looking for Eve. He said, "Adam, where are you?"

Your wife will be like a fruitful vine within your house;
your sons will be like olive shoots around your table.
Psalm 128:3 NIV

J U L Y   1 1

When your time comes to get married,
God will bring you someone with strengths
to complement your weaknesses.

_____

*Trust in the Lord with all your heart and
lean not on your own understanding.*
Proverbs 3:5 *NIV*

J U N E   2 3

In the past there were things we did not do simply because they were wrong. We as Christian parents can teach our children this is still true in our families.

Teach them the difference between what is holy and what is ordinary, what is pure and what is impure.
Leviticus 10:10 TLB

J U L Y   1 0

*M*arriage is a type, an illustration,
of Christ and the church.

---

*You wives must willingly obey your husbands in everything,
just as the Church obeys Christ. And you husbands,
show the same kind of love to your wives as Christ
showed the Church when he died for her.*
Ephesians 5:24,25 TLB

J U N E   2 4

A man of God is described in Job 29. Proverbs 31 describes a woman of God.

————————————————

I put on righteousness and it clothed me....
I was a father to the needy.
Job 29:14,16 NRSV

She opens her mouth with wisdom, and
the teaching of kindness is on her tongue.
Proverbs 31:26 NRSV

J U L Y   9

One of the best gifts a godly man can give his family is a sense of stability in this unstable world.

Stand firm. Let nothing move you. Always give yourselves fully to the work of the Lord.
1 Corinthians 15:58 NIV

JUNE 25

*T*here is greater hope for our culture if husbands and fathers will take back their leadership role.

Discipline your son, for in that there is hope.
Proverbs 19:18 NIV

J U L Y   8

The marriage covenant is a wonderful means for transferring blessing from one generation to another. My children are benefiting from the covenant faithfulness of my parents and my wife's parents to their marriages.

For the Lord is good and his love endures forever;
his faithfulness continues through all generations.
Psalm 100:5 NIV

J U N E   2 6

*W*hen Adam saw Eve, he realized that she was bone of his bone and flesh of his flesh. He realized that this was the start of a new kind of relationship.

———————————————

The man said, "This is now bone of my bones and flesh of my flesh; she shall be called 'woman' for she was taken out of man."
Genesis 2:23 NIV

J U L Y   7

*S*ome of the sweetest times you will ever have with your family are family devotion times. Dad, do not leave the devotions to your wife. Make them fun. Keep them interesting. But get started.

But the lovingkindness of the Lord is from everlasting to everlasting, to those who reverence him; his salvation is to children's children of those who are faithful to...him!
Psalm 103:17,18 TLB

JUNE 27

For a wife and mother, loving her home means deciding consciously that her home comes before everything else in the human sphere.

Encourage the young women to love their husbands, to love their children, to be... good managers of the household.
Titus 2:4 NRSV

J U L Y   6

*W*hoever first said this is right:
The best thing a father can do for
his children is to love their mother.

_____

Husbands, love your wives.
Colossians 3:19 NIV

J U N E   2 8

$\mathcal{T}$here is no government program that can fix a family if the father is not there.

_____

Fathers tell their children about your faithfulness.
Isaiah 38:19 NIV

J U L Y   5

A wife and mother should be held in the highest esteem in her home. A husband's job is to make sure his wife is respected, that no one sasses Mom without answering to Dad!

A child left to himself disgraces his mother.
Proverbs 29:15 NIV

J U N E   2 9

*P*arents today need wisdom, divine common sense, to fulfill the calling of God in their families.

―――――――――――――――

By wisdom a house is built, and by understanding it is established.
Proverbs 24:3 NRSV

J U L Y   4

A family is beautiful when the parents are living in covenant faithfulness and the children are obeying the covenant.

The Lord's love is with those who fear him, and his righteousness with their children's children—with those who keep his covenant.
Psalm 103:17,18 NIV

JUNE 30

*W*omen do not necessarily want to be liberated from male leadership, only from bad male leadership.

———————————————

He who loves his wife loves himself.
Ephesians 5:28 NIV

J U L Y   3

Marriage is a mutual yielding of everything that two people have, including their bodies.

The wife's body does not belong to her alone but also to her husband. In the same way, the husband's body does not belong to him alone but also to his wife.
1 Corinthians 7:4 NIV

J U L Y   1

$g$od intends mothers to have a dynamic influence in their homes, but not to usurp the influence of the father.

Listen, my son, to your father's instruction and do not forsake your mother's teaching.
Proverbs 1:8 NIV

J U L Y   2